1 A family of substance, *c.*1860s, assembled at the
front door: a favourite kind of Victorian photograph

2 *Overleaf* A picture of apparent rural benignity,
three generations and cats, but the interior
probably left much to be desired

S99559

LONDON BOROUGH OF ENFIELD
LIBRARY SERVICES

This book to be RETURNED on or before the latest date stamped unless a renewal has been obtained by personal call, post or telephone, quoting the above number and the date due for return.

The Victorian and Edwardian HOME from old photographs

Jenni Calder

B.T. Batsford Ltd
London

Acknowledgements

I would especially like to thank the staff of the People's Palace Museum, Glasgow, and Colin Harvey of the Heatherbank Museum, Milngavie, who gave up much of their time to assist me with this book. And thanks, too, to my daughter Rachel, who helped me sort and select the pictures.

The pictures have come from many different sources, and thanks is expressed for them: the Barnardo Photo Library, for nos 111, 113 and 114; the Beamish Museum Collection, for no. 122; Bideford Museum, for no. 63; Birmingham Public Library, for no. 62; Birmingham Reference Library, for nos 5, 26, 32, 82 (Stone Negatives); the Bodleian Library, for nos 56, 57; the Bodmin Museum, for no. 104; P.J. Brett, for no. 67; the Cambridge and County Folk Museum, for no. 102; Cambridgeshire Libraries, for no. 99; Chapman & Son, for no. 35; Mrs R.A. Crisp, for no. 29; Dartford Public Library, for no. 13; East Anglian Museum, Photographic Collection, for no. 79; Edinburgh Public Library (Grant Collection) for nos 38 and 93; Essex Record Office, for no. 117; Exeter City Library, for no. 90; Rev. C.J. Fowles, for no. 68; Mr F.J. Garrett and Mr M. Haird, for no. 97; Greater London Council, Photographic Unit, Department of Architecture and Civic Design, for no. 22; Green-Jaques, for no. 87; Hamilton Public Library, for no. 85; Hampshire County Museum Service, for no. 53; Harrogate Public Library, for no. 9; Heatherbank Museum of Social Work, for no. 116; Ironbridge Gorge Museum Trust, for no. 77; Mrs M.L. Jackson, for no. 2; the Jewsbury and Joiner Collection, Solihull, for no. 107; Kent County Library, for no. 16; Leamington Library, for no. 3; Leeds Public Library, for no. 18; Liverpool Corporation, City Engineers Department Photo Section, for nos 20 and 106; London Borough of Newham, Photographic Collection, Libraries Department, for nos 17 and 19; Miss F.M. McCormick, for no. 61; Museum of English Rural Life, University of Reading, for nos 91 and 110; National Monuments Record, for nos 6, 14 and 21; the National Museum of Wales, Welsh Folk Museum, for no. 96; Nuneaton Public Library, for no. 28; the People's Palace Museum, Glasgow, for nos 74, 86, 108 and 109; the Post Office, for nos 94 and 95; Radio Times Hulton Picture Library, for nos 40, 58, 71, 72 and 73; Reeves Collection, Sunday Times, for no. 76; Rothman Collection, for no. 33; School of Scottish Studies, Edinburgh University, for nos 39 and 92; the Science Museum, London, for no. 31; Shetland County Library, for no. 75; the J.H. Spalding Collection, for no. 1; Tonbridge Historical Society, for no. 63; Tunbridge Wells Public Library, for no. 11; Victoria and Albert Museum for nos 10, 43, 59, 69, 70, 78 and 80; Mr C. Washtell, for no. 98. Pictures 55 and 60 are reproduced by permission of Her Majesty The Queen.

ISBN 0 7134 0793 X
First published 1979
© in the text and compilation Jenni Calder 1979
Filmset in 'Monophoto' Apollo by
Servis Filmsetting Ltd, Manchester
Printed in Great Britain by the Anchor Press Ltd
Tiptree, Essex
for the Publishers B.T. Batsford Ltd,
4 Fitzhardinge Street, London W1H 0AH

Contents

3 The library of Moreton Lodge, Leamington, 1900. The heavily patterned carpet and wallpaper and the crowding of pictures on the wall and objects on the mantelpiece were characteristic of mid-Victorian decoration

Introduction

One of the delights of looking back at the Victorians and Edwardians is that, although in attitudes and behaviour they may seem very distant and different from ourselves, they are in fact so very accessible. The printed word is part of the accessibility, the novels and journalism that poured forth from so many accomplished pens; but crucial also is the camera, an aid to understanding that previous periods were without. Photographs amplify and crystallise much of what we read about. The visual impression is very important, especially as a record of a time when appearances accounted for a great deal.

The Victorians and Edwardians cared very much about the way their homes looked, as well as about the life that went on within them. Taste was discussed a great deal in the Victorian period, and there were many who concerned themselves with it, from cultural giants like John Ruskin to anonymous writers in women's magazines who instructed mainly middle-class housewives about the colour of paint they should choose, the patterns on their carpets and the objects on their mantel shelves. Although perhaps to us now the Victorians seem distinctly lacking in what we would think of as 'good taste', inclined as they were to crowd their rooms with bulky furniture and cover every surface with useless artefacts – surfaces were often created precisely in order to be covered with not very decorative objects – good taste in home-making was considered to be of the highest importance. A family, and especially the wife and mother, was often judged by the objects the home contained and the way they were arranged. Tastefulness, along with the efficient running of the home, was regarded as vital. An education in taste was considered to be essential for the potential home maker.

At the height of the Victorian period, let's say around the 1860s, taste was felt to be not just an expression of aesthetic judgment, but primarily a moral quality. Your drawing room revealed your worth, your economic worth obviously, but more importantly (though they were often allied in the Victorian mind) your moral worth. This was of course a very middle-class concern, and partly the result of the middle classes – being a relatively new and rapidly growing section of society – still feeling some insecurity. They had on one side the landed and still very much the governing class, which was quite confident of its place and value; and on the other the vast and disturbing working classes, which seemed to constitute a physical and a moral threat. Middle-class money could not always make up for middle-class lack of confidence and security. Though it tried. One of the reasons that we tend to think of the Victorian period as being the age of middle-class dominance – and the Edwardian as expressing the flowering of middle-class leisure – is that the middle class was so very concerned to establish its value and values, the result of uncertainty about both.

But we won't find the uncertainty expressed directly in the home, in the way that we can find it brilliantly portrayed by the great Victorian novelists. What we do find is the attempt to build up an environment of comfort and security, a place of safety to which the family can retreat and forget about the difficult and dangerous world outside. Tastefulness became wrapped up in the need for security. It is difficult not to see the heavy furniture and the drapery, the dark colours and the enormous plant pots, often ranged along the window sill keeping out the light, and by inference the outside world also, as part of the attempt to create a bulwark against intrusion. The world outside was indeed not a pleasant one, especially in the cities, which grew at a speed that could not be controlled or coped with. The dirt, the smells, the primitive sewage disposal, the dubious water supplies, the disease, the economic facts of a highly competitive world, these are things we need to bear in mind and which photographs cannot so easily suggest – though some of the pictures of working-class homes do, I think, convey intimations of these. Part of the reason for the dark comfort of the mid-Victorian financially secure home was the bare squalor of so many others.

The stark contrast was never eliminated by either Victorians or Edwardians, though many cared deeply about the improvement of living conditions and managed to do something about them in some of the most crowded and delapidated urban areas. And there was no void between the two. There were vast numbers of homes that, with a very small income and very hard work, attained the standards of neatness and decency that the middle classes approved. Cherished objects were most lovingly displayed in the humblest homes. There were changes in attitude towards the home, which these photographs reflect. By the 1870s the more thoughtful writers on taste and home management were criticising the over-stuffed tendency and encouraging a move towards changes in design. Even before this William Morris and those associated with him were reacting against mass production which, although it made many things cheaply and easily available, Morris considered to be soul-destroying for maker and owner alike. He preferred the personal and loving touch of the craftsman.

Morris's ideas and designs were part of a general lightening of attitude and effect. Ironically, improvements in machine techniques also aided this. Paper making, for instance, had become much cheaper, so wallpaper became more common, which offered an opportunity for more colour and interest in design. Morris's wallpapers were amongst the most notable. Other improvements helped to change the look of the insides of homes. The introduction of gas first and then electricity brought a revolution in methods of heating and lighting. By the end of the century gas cookers, a novelty in the Great Exhibition of 1851, were common, much cleaner and easier to use than the old kitchen ranges. Gas lighting was at first very noisy and smelly, but it was improved rapidly, and by the middle of the century a network of gas mains served many urban areas. By the end of the century electricity was beginning to take over. This brought the introduction of labour-saving devices, such as vacuum cleaners and kitchen gadgets. Dark colours, partly explained by the need to camouflage encroaching dirt, were less necessary. An immense interest in oriental design, which began in the 1870s and was fostered by designers like Morris and some shops, especially Liberty's which was initially established to sell oriental goods, also encouraged the move towards lighter interiors. Paler colours, more graceful shapes, the use of bamboo and cane, the vogue for a less heavy, more flowing effect in drapery, were characteristic of the oriental influence.

There were architects too who strongly reacted against what we think of as characteristically Victorian. The terrace housing of the inner urban areas, the semi-detached villas of speedy suburban growth, were generally put up by speculative builders who did not concern themselves much with overall planning, and simply

4 At Caversham, Berkshire, *c.*1895

repeated accepted designs. It is true that the most memorable Victorian architects tended to be busy with town halls, government buildings, railway stations and churches; we don't think of the average private house as featuring amongst the grandiosity of Victorian building. But there were architects who were much concerned with the design of the home, and the houses they built help us to chart the extent of the change of attitude towards the home. Architects like Philip Webb, who built the Red House for William Morris, and Norman Shaw, who created, amongst numerous other London houses, Bedford Park, an example of total planning in suburban development, were concerned to free the home environment from some of the weightier pressures that tended to characterise it. By the Edwardian period, in the hands of such as C.F.A. Voysey and Charles Rennie Mackintosh the home had become a much freer and more open environment. A plainer, much less ornate style was what these two designers produced, with simple contrasts of colour and shape. Instead of covering up as much as possible, with curtains and drapes and artefacts, they were inclined to strip as much as possible, to rely on basic colours, often black and white, to expose beams, to repeat selected shapes in design, to abolish clutter. Taste began to be seen as a combination of the elegant and the utilitarian.

But of course only a few homes reflected these changes in any significant way. Innovations generally required money as well as a change of attitude. Many of the photographs in this collection show the homes of middle-class families at the turn of

5 Bourneville: an interior of *c.* 1895

the century which still seem to be characteristically Victorian. We can detect some influences that had an effect fairly quickly. It is easy, for instance, to change your wallpaper or your curtains or the colour of your paint, so innovations in design in these features can be more readily detected. But to change your furniture, or your carpets, or even your habits of twenty years or so, is a much bigger business. Fashion plates and furniture catalogues may reflect an ideal of sorts, but photographs help to show us what ordinary people looked like in their ordinary homes. People of course wanted to look their best for the photographer, and early photographs in particular have an air of best clothes and formality about them. And taking a photograph was not the casual, quick flick of the shutter business it has become; it was an event. The tendency to stage photographs and the rigid posing were partly the result of the novelty of photography, partly due to the fact that it was often a serious and lengthy process.

The home and the family could be imposing symbols. It was in the Victorian period that ideas about the home came into the forefront of thinking about the way people should live. Many eminent Victorian thinkers had something to say about the way the home should be run and the quality of home life. The home was regarded as a place of refuge in which comfort and security were the main objects. Almost inevitably it was closed and inward looking. It was considered to be the main role of women to maintain this refuge. In the home women and children could be protected from the hard facts of the world outside, and men could rest from their labours and for a while forget about them. This was the ideal, at least. For many the hardest facts of life ruled their home existence. For the privileged, the lightening of design in the home meant a lightening of atmosphere, and that in turn reflects a much more open attitude to the home and life within it. This certainly had something to do with the changing status of women, who became less likely to lead most of their lives within the walls of their own homes, and more likely to have centres of interest outside, but it also had a great deal to do with a reaction against 'Victorianism', which began long before the death of Victoria.

It is misleading, though, to see life in the Victorian home as totally confined and repressed. Some of the photographs here suggest something quite different, lively games, the garden as much the location of family life as the inside, all kinds of activities, and a great deal of very hard work. The middle- and upper-class home was dependent on servants to keep it running. Victorian houses were most frequently designed with very little thought of ease of management. For the wife and mother who was also housekeeper the maintenance of even a minimum of decency in a home that lacked space and amenities was an incessant task. Often, too, in spite of the vast extension of machine labour, the home was the place where livings were earned. Traditionally, many kinds of piece work had been done in the home, weaving and knitting, glove making and lace making, often performed by very young children,

6   Croquet on the lawn at 'Beechmont', Sevenoaks, c.1860

and some of these were continued, particularly in rural and remote areas, until well into the twentieth century.

Running a home became easier in many ways with the increase in amenities and services. In the early part of the Victorian period piped water was a luxury, and drainage was extremely primitive, even in respectable residential areas. Gradually there were improvements. Builders and architects began to realise that such things as water supply and sewage disposal had to be accommodated in their building and planning, but more effective, although painfully slow to come, were the improvements in drainage made by local authorities, after Edwin Chadwick's Public Health Act of 1848. But under-privileged areas lived with open drains and standpipes from which water had to be fetched – and the supply was often only turned on two or three times a week – well into the Edwardian period. The water was often polluted, and where it was not, the problem of keeping clean and free from disease when every drop of water had to be carried, often a considerable distance, was immense. The problem was enhanced by the fact that in many areas privies were shared, and were often again at some distance from the homes they served.

A full scale bathroom was a luxury in even quite opulent homes, but by the last twenty years of the century bathrooms were usually built into new middle-class housing, properly equipped and often with delightfully ornate fittings. Gas and electricity meant that the provision of hot water for the bathroom did not need to be dependent on a kitchen range or the labour of servants. The achievement of instant hot water out of a tap was without a doubt the most significant aspect of domestic progress. Central heating was very slow to catch on in Britain, although it was often discussed and was well established in America, but at least many households were able to move beyond a dependence on coal.

It was not only sources of water and fuel that were revolutionised. There were great changes in methods of manufacture. Mass production meant that a great variety of items became generally available and fairly cheap. Glass and china, for instance, could now be produced on a very large scale. New materials were being experimented with, cast iron, steel, later plastic. This was one of the reasons why the Victorians tended to have so many things in the home; there simply were so many more things available than there had been. Much of what was produced was virtually useless and not perhaps to us particularly decorative, but the Victorians were fascinated with the ornate, and equated it with moral status. Although the Edwardians moved away from this tendency, they retained a belief in the desirability of decoration that was more than functional. It was aesthetic values that mattered, and an expression of individual personality. The importance of these in the reaction against Victorianism was to be seen in every aspect of culture.

Services also contributed immensely to changes in home life. A feature of the rapid urban expansion of the Victorian period was the building of vast tracts of residential housing with very little in the way of shops in the immediate vicinity. So deliveries were of great importance. (Allied to this was the middle-class reluctance to shop

7   An Edwardian drawing room in Kensington, designed by Leonard R. Wyburd

personally, especially to the extent of carrying home shopping.) The butcher, the baker, the coal merchant, had traditionally delivered to the middle classes. By the end of the century there were laundries, department stores, dairies, the postal service of course. Practically anything could be delivered. And there were telephones, too, in a few households, so it was possible for some to get all they required without stirring from the home. Having an account was the accepted way for anyone with any status.

For the majority for whom it was necessary to go out to shop there was in most cities a system of public transport that was growing all the time. Horse buses and trams gave way to electric trams and trolleys. London's underground was begun in the 1880s, and the suburban lines on the railways meant that those living in the new outer suburbs of London could get to Regent Street and Oxford Street, by the 1860s well established as London's major shopping centre, easily and quickly. There, in Swan and Edgar's or Peter Robinson's or Liberty's, for the more exotic, the housewife could purchase whatever she considered necessary for her home. In Tottenham Court Road the great furniture stores Maple's and Shoolbred's supplied thousands of homes with every variety of furniture, and Heal's supplied those with a more modern taste in design.

The value of the home was reflected in countless ways. Although most Victorians did not own their homes, for it was customary to rent rather than to buy, especially in the cities, the importance of the ownership of the property within was fundamental. The way your home looked was a way of demonstrating your economic and your moral worth, and both were at the heart of much of what we think of as a typically Victorian outlook. If the Edwardians were more concerned with demonstrating an aesthetic sense, a different kind of worth, and to express personality rather than substance through their homes, they were just as concerned with appearances. The reaction against mass production, initiated by Morris and carried on by the Arts and Crafts movement, was greatly concerned with the way things looked, even though it placed so much emphasis on the care and commitment that went into their making. There were those who felt that ownership should imply not the materialistic display of property, which was considered crude and in bad taste, but a perpetuation of this care and commitment. But it was impossible to escape judgment from appearances.

However, the fulfilment of both the Victorian ideal and the Edwardian reaction was a luxury. The vast majority could not afford to think so much about what their homes should contain or even about how they should be run. There were many who had no choice in these matters, and many who had no homes at all. The problem of the homeless and the destitute was a very large one, and there was considerable conflict of opinion over how it should be dealt with. The totally destitute could be provided with a roof and a bed in the workhouse, for which they were expected to pay with labour, but the indignity of this meant that many resisted it. Nevertheless the workhouse was home for a substantial number, as were other kinds of institutions. Provision for homeless and parentless children who were not 'on the parish' was in private hands.

8   A Dartmoor cottage kitchen, 1890

Dr Barnardo is the best known of those who attempted to house just a few of the thousands of homeless children. Lodging houses were often home for the indigent, and they were grim and depressing places. At the other end of the scale there were the substitute homes for the many children who were sent away to school, boarding schools of all kinds, from the renowned public schools to small and often dubious establishments, all of them likely to counteract any idea of cosy domesticity.

For a large proportion of the population home was not a place of comfort and privacy, a territory of private and personal authority, but a place of subjection to the rules and whims of others. For many of those who occupied and ran their own homes, it was necessity that governed the nature of their homes, not choice, or idealism. The nature of the home, values themselves, depended on employment and wages, on luck perhaps, and although the middle classes urged hard work and discipline on the working classes, and were anxious to teach cleanliness and good housekeeping, it could be a soul-destroying task for the working-class housewife to keep her home homely.

I have arranged this collection of photographs under eight headings, in an attempt to give some idea of what 'home' could mean to the Victorians and Edwardians. The sections on Housing, Interiors and Design suggest something of the visual quality of the home, and how it changed, from the 1850s to the second decade of the twentieth century. The sections on Work, the Garden and Family Life it is hoped will give some impression of life in the home, and the section on Services and Amenities indicates some of the developments that affected home life. The section on Institutions reminds us that there were those for whom the home was not the conventional, domestic setting, but something rather bleaker and less personal.

Fortunately for us, the Victorians and Edwardians had an immense interest in documenting their lives. The Victorians in particular loved facts and loved detail. The camera was an incomparably appropriate instrument for them, for it enabled them to record both quickly and authentically. Although many nineteenth-century artists and illustrators incorporated an immense amount of domestic detail into their pictures, and many writers into novels and essays, the camera was justly valued for its documentary powers and was often used with the greatest care and deliberation. Whether we are looking at a wealthy family relaxing on a spacious lawn, or children starving in an East End slum, or a carefully posed occupant of a carefully arranged drawing room, each picture offers us a moment of truth. Each picture, as well as often being a delight to the eye, gives us a clue, however minute, to the way we were.

Housing

9 A solid, substantial dwelling, clearly occupied
by solid, substantial people

10 *Overleaf* Gordon Castle, Fochabers, *c.*1890.
An imposing country seat, though the land-owning
classes sometimes had problems in maintaining such
establishments

11 Grosvenor Lodge, Tunbridge Wells. The
conservatory is characteristically Victorian

12 Victorian villa with an irresistible Gothic
flourish

13   Dartford Vicarage, *c*.1910. The small town or
country vicarage often suggests an Edwardian ideal.
The impression here is of untroubled, pleasant
security

14   Typical Victorian suburban terrace housing, Fulham

15   Similar housing going up

16   A residential street in Folkestone. A middle-
class housing development of the latter part of the
nineteenth century

18 *Overleaf*   A Leeds court. The innocent looking
gutter in the centre of the lane was probably in
effect an open sewer

17   Basic housing, Canning Town, 1900

19 Improved housing in London. A slight touch of ornamentation relieves the heavily utilitarian aspect

20 The backs of working-class houses in Liverpool, 1911

21 Lever Street, Finsbury, 1893. The construction
of special housing for the working classes by
organisations other than employers began in the
late 1840s. The best known are probably the
Peabody Buildings, financed by money from George
Peabody, who died in 1869

22   Millbank Estate. Municipal building came late
on the scene

23 Port Sunlight, near Liverpool. A paternalistic
development built for their workers by Lever
Brothers in 1886

24 The exteriors were often picturesque, but
rural slums were a great problem, and received less
attention than the more glaring urban situation

Interiors

25 The draped mantel was a common feature of the Victorian drawing room. 1893

26 An unpretentious parlour, probably in a
country home

27 Typical Victorian display. The plants, the vases, the ornamental clock, the stands on the mantelpiece to hold yet more ornament, all approved by Victorian taste

28 South Farm, Arbury where George Eliot was born. The design of the wallpaper and drapery suggests William Morris. China dogs were favourite Victorian ornaments

29 An Oxford drawing room, 1904, with a heavily carved pedestal table in the right foreground. The photograph in the corner is probably of a dead child

30 In many households mid-Victorian heavy
drapery and cluttered walls lasted well into the
twentieth century

31 An 1880s bathroom. Still a luxury at that time,
but deemed suitable for unstinted ornamentation

32 In Bourneville, the creation of chocolate paternalism,
a tip-up bath is provided in the kitchen. *c*.1910

33 The Winter Garden at Somerleyton Hall, 1890.
The use of glass and iron as building materials
encouraged the construction of conservatories,
winter gardens and greenhouses

34 Kitchens remained largely functional in appearance. Here there is a gas cooker, fairly common in the last quarter of the nineteenth century, next to a kitchen range

A COTTAGE HOME. DARTMOOR

35 A more primitive cottage kitchen – but drapery and display are still important

36 Farm kitchen, with settle and dresser on which the best china and glass is displayed, probably amongst the household's most prized possessions

37 This Cornish cottage, 1909, with
beautiful scrollwork on the kitchen
range, is rather more sophisticated
than the croft in the next photograph

38 A croft interior, 1880s. Furniture of the most
basic kind, and an open fire to cook on

39 A Lanarkshire
weaver's cottage, *c*.1890,
reflecting a basic and bare
existence

40   A slum interior in the East End, 1912. The
flowered wallpaper and scraps of decoration only
highlight the evidence of dirt and disintegration

Design

41 Cadogan Square, London. A splendid example
of the Victorian delight in ornamentation. Designed
by the firm of Ernest George and Peto and built in
1886

42   The Red House, Bexley Heath, designed by
Philip Webb to suit the needs and interests of
William Morris, completed in 1861

43 The Red House. Morris and his friends
designed and decorated the interior and the
furniture

44 Queen's Gate, London, designed by Norman
Shaw and built in 1896. A move away from
the Victorian heyday of the over-stuffed interior

45 Another example of the retreat from Victorian clutter. Unfussy, more utilitarian furniture was part of the reaction. George Walton, architect, *c.*1906

46 Dickhurst, Haslemere, designed by C.
Harrison Townsend, *c.*1906. The influence of
Morris and of the Arts and Crafts movement is
evident here, in the exposed beams, the austerely
carved mantel and furniture, and the careful but
unburdened arrangement

7 The Old Swan House, Chelsea, one of Norman Shaw's London houses. 1877

48 *Overleaf* Bryanston, Dorset. A country house by Norman Shaw, with a Jacobean flavour. 1890

49   In contrast, a good example of Victorian Gothic:
Eaton Hall, Cheshire, designed by Alfred
Waterhouse, *c.*1867. Money gained through trade
and manufacture often went into such splendid
homes

50 Charles Rennie Mackintosh was one of the most original and interesting of the late Victorian and Edwardian designers. These interiors show his characteristic geometric style. *c.*1906

51 Designed by C.F.A. Voysey c.1906: a late Victorian architect who believed in a simple and practical environment for daily life

52 Edwardian housing in Skegness which reflects the new trends in design

The Garden

53 Mid-Victorian ladies at leisure in the garden,
with the necessary mid-Victorian gardeners
assembled, complete with magnificent lawn mower

54 The garden of Lacock Abbey, early 1840s. This photograph has a striking Gothic quality, a result partly of the style of architecture and partly of the darkness and slight blur

55 5th November, 1853. Queen Victoria's enthusiasm for Scotland brought tartans into fashion

56 A game of hunt the slipper in an Oxford garden, 1857. Hats and a summer house were protection from the sun

57 The same family playing lawn billiards

58 Charles Dickens reading to his daughters in the garden of Gadshill, his house in Kent, *c*.1869

60 Queen Mary took this picture in 1899. Lady Katherine Coke uses a box camera

61 A Cambridge garden, in a pleasant and prosperous residential street

62 A Northumberland garden, 1902. Behind the
flower bed there is a croquet lawn

63 Croquet, a game that ladies and gentlemen
could play together, became popular in the middle
of the nineteenth century. The open upstairs
windows indicate bedrooms airing

65 *Overleaf*   Bowls, another game for a large garden. Towards the end of the nineteenth century great emphasis was placed on the healthfulness of fresh air and exercise

64   Croquet in rural Devon, 1874. It was to take more energetic sports to bring about modifications in women's dress, although in the 1870s the bustle took over from the crinoline

66 Tennis became popular in the 1880s. In this late-Victorian rectory garden there is room for both tennis and croquet

Family Life

67 Music in the drawing room with mama, a very suitable activity for the young. A photograph by John Brett, ARA, of his wife and children, *c.*1880

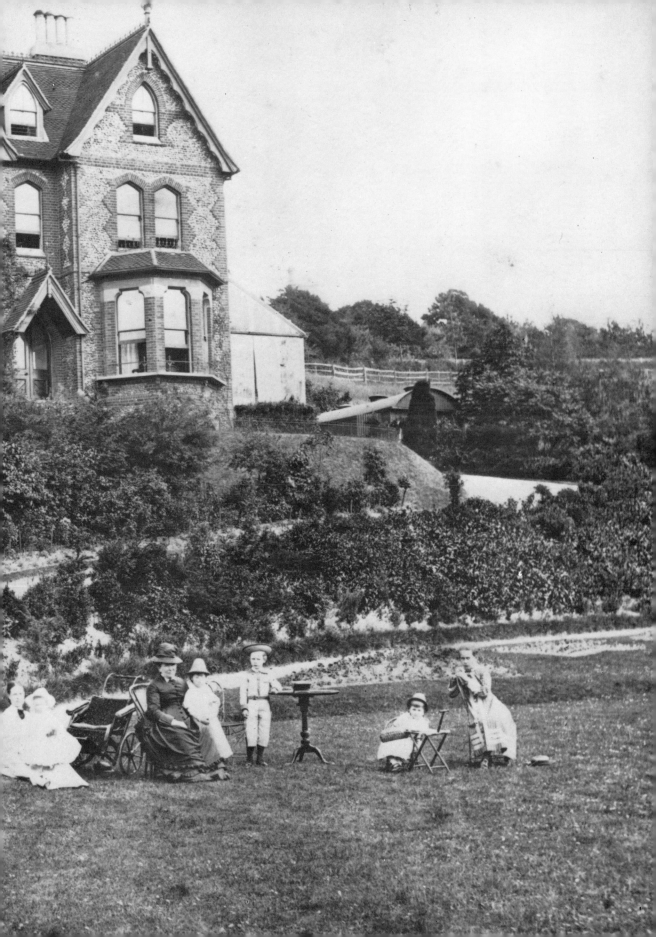

69   Tea in the garden. Mother and daughters, perhaps, in the 1890s

68 *Previous page*   A substantial mid-Victorian villa, with a substantial Victorian family enjoying the garden. Mrs Whitfield, with five of her ten children, a maid and a gardener, Surrey, 1876

70 A middle-class family at dinner, probably the 1860s. A picture that appears to be pleasantly unposed

71 A more formal tea time, in the 1860s, though the stiffness here is probably due to the long exposure necessary for an interior shot

72 An East End family, 1912. In spite of the
impressive array of china and glass these children
have nothing to eat

73 An East End slum interior, 1912. Probably the
family's only room

74 It was an unquestioned necessity of working-class life that children should care for younger siblings. The lucky ones had shoes. Calton, Glasgow, 1890s

76 *Overleaf*   The family on display, attended by servants, and a three-wheeled perambulator, *c.*1875

75   Cottage industries very often dominated family life, especially in remote areas. Here, in Scotland around 1900, a fisherman reads the newspaper under his catch, strung up to smoke, and the women of the house work

77 Wife and children greet the return of the master of the house from his obviously successful shooting, *c.*1865

78 A leisured group of Charles Dickens's family and friends at Gadshill, Kent, in the late 1860s. Dickens is the bearded figure lying on the ground at the right

Work

79 Cook and kitchen maids in a well-equipped late-Victorian kitchen. Domestic service accounted for the largest proportion of women in employment

80 *Overleaf* A formidable array of mid-Victorian servants. Housekeeper, butler and cook are probably the three in the centre. There seem to be three married couples

81 Every Victorian or Edwardian family that could be called middle-class had at least a housemaid

82   Maids hanging out washing, Stratford, 1899

83 A large country house kitchen. Upper-class eating was of course totally dependent on this kind of labour in the kitchen

84 In many rural areas a piped water supply was a luxury. In 1905 Sutton, Surrey had not yet become one of London's outer suburbs

Scrubbing steps, Calton, Glasgow, 1890s.
child's job

Edinburgh, 1890s. The arduous job of the
nily wash

87 Peeling potatoes in a Warwickshire farm yard,
1890

88 A gipsy family preparing dinner

89 Knitting socks in Wales. In many rural areas the economy was dependent on home industries

90 Lace making, another cottage industry.
Although the lace maker here is elderly, before the
1870 Education Act very young children were
taught the craft and expected to spend many hours
a day at it

93 Thatching was an essential craft in the
maintenance of many homes. The Hebrides, 1880s

Services and Amenities

94 London postman, 1903. The rapid improvement
of communications in general had a striking effect
on home life

96   Until late in the nineteenth century wood and coal fires were the only forms of heating, and chimney sweeping was an essential service

95 *Previous page*   In spite of the railway, horse-drawn Parcel Coaches were still used after the turn of the century. This is the London to Chatham coach about to make its last journey: June 1908

97 Carrier's cart, 1905. Although the railways revolutionised communications, many parts of the country depended on horse-drawn delivery until the motor car became common

98 Cambridgeshire milkman, *c.*1910. Milk delivery was a long-established service

99 Ely Fire Brigade, 1904. Municipal fire
brigades began to be established in the 1860s.
Before that fire brigades had been privately run, or
dependent on volunteers

100 The bicycle was one of the handiest aspects of
the communications revolution. It certainly aided
women's independence

101 *Overleaf* Picturesquely framed by a gothic
arch, but a less efficient means of getting about:
a donkey cart

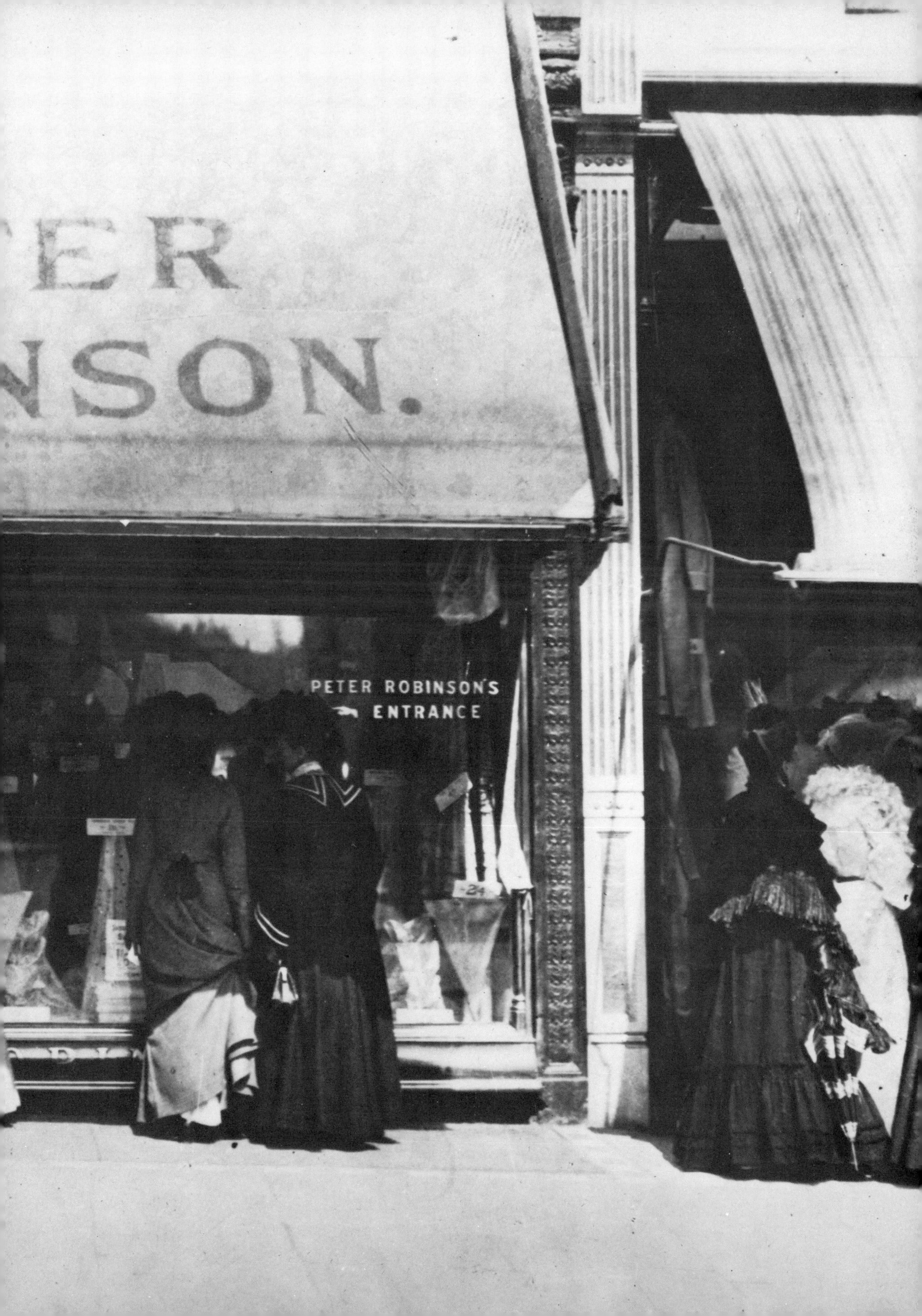
ER
NSON.
PETER ROBINSON'S
ENTRANCE

103 The local shop and post office was indispensable in areas where it was difficult or uncustomary to travel any distance for essentials

104 A Cornish chemist shop. The nineteenth century was the great age of the patent cure

105 In Edinburgh the fishwife from Newhaven who carried her basket of fish from house to house was a well-known figure

102 *Previous page* Regent Street shopping, 1905. The development of the department store revolutionised urban shopping in the second half of the nineteenth century, and helped to make a great variety of goods available to the home maker

106   A Liverpool court in 1906 where one pump
served all the surrounding homes. Water supply,
perhaps the amenity we now take most for granted,
was the cause of much contention in the Victorian
period

107 Soft water seller, Solihull High Street, *c.*1870.
In some parts of the country soft water was a prized
commodity

108 Glasgow, 1890s. The poor could not expect
coal delivery, and most could only afford as much
as could be carried

109 In crowded urban areas with few facilities a
local 'Patent Mangle' was a great asset in getting
through the weekly wash. Glasgow, 1890s

110 The final stage in the transport revolution.
Herefordshire, 1900

Institutions

111 Dr Barnardo is the best known of those who
concerned themselves with the plight of destitute
children. His principle was that no child should be
refused admittance from the homes

112   The Foundling Hospital, one of the earliest
institutions for the care of orphans

113 Not a reformatory, but a means of getting children off the streets and organised to do some kind of useful and remunerative work

114 Mealtime in a Barnardo home. Institutional uniformity was inevitable

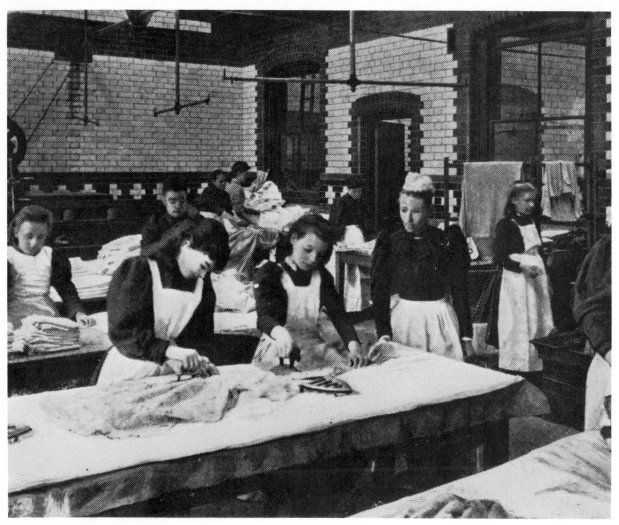

115 A fundamental principle of nineteenth-century
children's homes was work. Here girls work in the
Stockwell Orphanage laundry, aiding the running of
the home and learning a skill

116 A children's home in Lancashire, run by
Methodists, in 1871

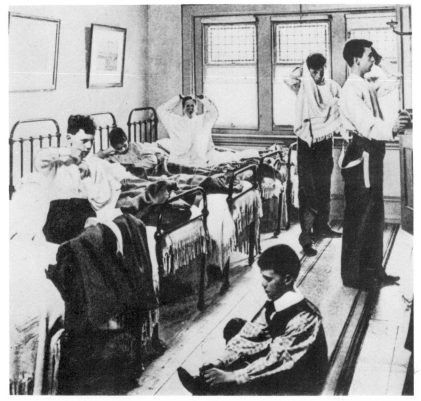

117 A dormitory at King
Edward VI School, Chelmsford
1907. For the privileged, but not
so different from the orphanage
dormitory in the next photograph

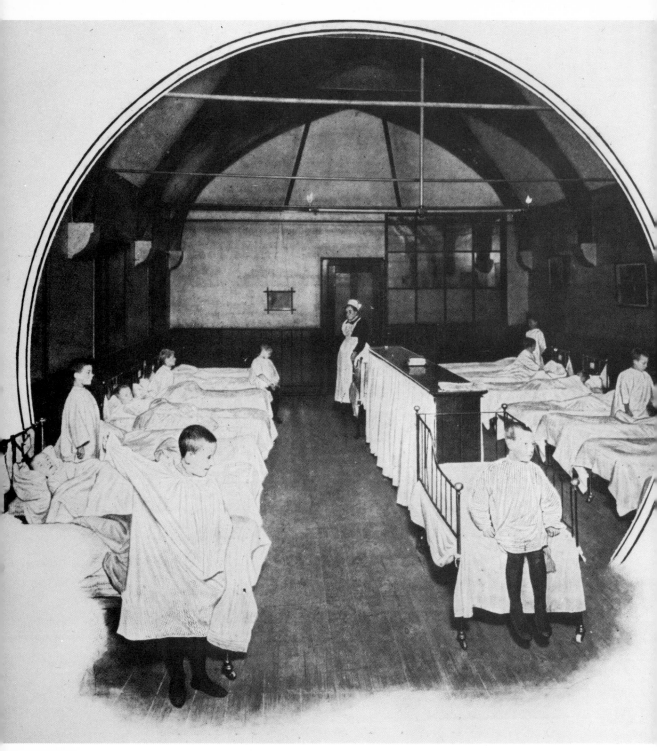

118   Bedtime at the Alexandra Orphanage,
Hornsey. *c.*1900

119 Provision for destitute adults was often evangelical. Here cocoa is served after a ragged church service, *c.*1902

120 A Rowton House, providing cheap lodgings
for the indigent, *c.*1900

121 Boys at Winchester College, 1866. The sons of the privileged were expected to do without the softer aspects of domestic life

122   The child's image of home has changed little.
These children were probably never inside a house
like the one this little girl painted